FINN'S

LITTLE

Fibs

DAIAN BOOKS

In the heart of a vibrant forest, where the trees whispered secrets to anyone who would listen, lived a young fox named Finn.

Finn was known for his
bright red coat and
even brighter tales.

Every day was an adventure with Finn, as he darted through the woods, playing hide-and-seek with his friends, and concocting exciting stories.

One sunny afternoon, while playing near the riverbank with his best friend, a cheerful rabbit named Ruby, Finn accidentally stepped on Ruby's favorite toy boat, cracking it slightly.

Worried about Ruby's reaction, Finn quickly thought of a story.

"It wasn't me!" Finn exclaimed as Ruby approached.

"I saw a big, clumsy bear stumble through here and step on your boat!"

Ruby looked puzzled
but believed Finn's tale.

However, Finn's little fib didn't feel as heroic as his usual stories.

A twinge of guilt pinched at his heart, but he pushed it aside, hoping the problem would just go away.

As the days passed, Finn's tiny fib began to grow bigger.

The story of the bear spread among the forest animals, and Finn kept adding details to make it more believable.

Each time he told the story, he felt the weight of his words heavier on his heart.

Ruby, meanwhile, was growing wary of the forest paths, always on the lookout for the imaginary clumsy bear.

Finn noticed that Ruby didn't laugh as much and seemed more anxious during their games.

Seeing his friend's distress, Finn felt even worse.

One sunny morning, while gathering berries with his friends, Finn overheard Ruby expressing her fear of wandering too far in case the bear returned.

Finn's heart sank as
he realized how his lie
had affected
his friend.

Feeling the burden of his dishonesty, Finn decided it was time to set things right.

That evening, he gathered all his friends around the old oak tree, the heart of their little community.

With all the courage he could muster, Finn stepped forward.

"I have something important to tell you all," Finn began, his voice shaky.

"There is no clumsy bear. I was the one who broke Ruby's toy boat."

"I made up the story because I was scared of losing my friend."

A silence fell over the group. Finn looked at Ruby, her eyes wide with surprise.

"I'm really sorry, Ruby," he continued. "I was wrong to lie. It was just easier than telling the truth."

Ruby took a moment, then hopped closer to Finn.

"Thank you for telling us the truth, Finn. I forgive you, but I was really scared of that bear," she said with a small smile.

"Let's not let lies scare us anymore."

Finn felt a wave of relief wash over him as his friends nodded in agreement.

From that day on, Finn learned the value of honesty. He realized that the truth might be difficult to tell sometimes, but it was always better than a lie that could hurt the ones he loved.

The forest returned
to its cheerful rhythm,
with all the animals
playing and laughing
together, their trust in
Finn restored.

And Finn, with his heart a little lighter, made sure his adventures were truly honest.

The End.

HONESTY IS THE BEST POLICY